The Infinity Inside

Jewish Spiritual Practice through a Multi-faith Lens

Rabbi Laura Duhan-Kaplan

Boulder, Colorado
2019

"The old shall be renewed,
and the new shall be made holy."
— Rabbi Avraham Yitzhak Kook

Albion-Andalus, Inc.
P. O. Box 19852
Boulder, CO 80308
www.albionandalus.com

Design and composition by Erica Holland Leitz
Cover design by D.A.M. Cool Graphics
Front cover and artwork by Rodolphe Parfait

Manufactured in the United States of America

ISBN-10: 1-7336589-4-7

ISBN-13: 978-1-7336589-4-2

For my children, Hillary and Eli
who easily blend
the spirituality of art and nature
with the best of their religious tradition

Table of Contents

Acknowledgments

Many great teachers from various spiritual traditions helped me discover the ideas in this book. My rabbinic guides include Rabbi Marcia Prager, Dean of ALEPH Ordination Programs; Rabbi Miles Krassen, my rabbinic studies director; and our shared teacher Rabbi Zalman Schachter-Shalomi, *z"l*. Among Christian teachers, I particularly wish to thank Sheilla Fodchuck, human rights activist and spirituality educator at the Vancouver School of Theology; and her close friend Dr. Bonnelle Strickling, psychotherapist, philosopher, and my long-time spiritual director. I am grateful for my training in Yoga with Loretta Levitz and David Liberty of Boston's Ayurvedic Rehabilitation Center and their mentor, Dr. Vasant Lad.

Many learning communities helped me explore the ideas more deeply. They include the New Life Centre, University of North Carolina at Charlotte, Havurat Tikvah, ALEPH: Alliance for Jewish Renewal, Or Shalom Synagogue, Grind Café and Gallery, Multi-Faith Action Society, Vancouver School of Theology, Naramata Centre, Limmud Vancouver, Intention Gathering, VST's Indigenous Studies Program, Canadian Memorial United Church and Centre for Peace, West Vancouver United Church, and Bethlehem Centre. Thanks to graphic designer Rodolphe Parfait, whom I met at the Intention Gathering, for the cover art.

Three people in particular helped me shape the ideas into this short book. Rabbi Rebecca Sirbu, former director of Rabbis Without Borders, encouraged me to begin blogging about spirituality. Dr. Charles Kaplan, my beloved spouse, carefully read early drafts of every chapter for content and clarity. Netanel Miles-Yépez, publisher at Albion-Andalus Books, brings a broad vision of spirituality to his work. His clarity and flexibility helped bring this book into print.

Finally, I am grateful to the Spirit that animates everyone listed above.

— Laura Duhan-Kaplan
Vancouver, British Columbia, Canada, 2018
Unceded territories of the Musqueam, Squamish, and Tsleil-Waututh Nations

Introduction

✵

Inside each of us, there is a portal to the infinite. We might call it soul, spirit, psyche, intuition, or imagination. As children, we often walk through it easily. But as adults, we might need to re-learn, explicitly, how to do so. Thus, this short book offers an introduction to contemplative spiritual practices. If you simply read the book, you might finish it in an hour. But if you experiment with the techniques, and reflect on the ideas, it might take you several years to finish "reading."

Some contemplative practices, like spending time in beautiful outdoor areas, cut across cultures. You don't need a special vocabulary. Only access, attention, and awareness. Others, like Sufi chanting, or meditating on the Hebrew words of the Shema, are culturally specific. As you participate, you gain cultural knowledge. Not just about theology, but about different ways of knowing your spirit. As a lifelong spiritual seeker, I have learned the ways of Kabbalah, western philosophy, Ayurvedic yoga, Christian spiritual direction, and depth psychology. Today, I integrate these paths in my work as Director of Inter-Religious Studies and Professor of Jewish Studies at the Vancouver School of Theology. In this book, I share that integrated perspective with you.

I begin by describing the challenge of opening to spiritual traditions. Then, I report on a walk in the woods that helps me define both "religion" and "spirituality." Next, I specify what I mean by spiritual practice. Then, I present ten different practices that I have learned from various traditions, especially Judaism, Christianity, and Yoga. All are practices I have explored intensively over many years. Thus, my presentations are personal and interpretive, as my own teachers have always encouraged them to be. The practices include focused breathing, labyrinth walking, chanting, developing intuition, praying with beads, examining conscience throughout the day, praying a formal liturgy, bringing blessing through loving action, and contemplating key words. Finally, I raise questions about the transformative role of spiritual practice, and close with a prayerful theological reflection. Into the book's presentation, I weave poetry, philosophy, and personal experiences.

Several historical Jewish celebrities inspired the poetry and philosophy. Spiritual poet Solomon ibn Gabirol (1021-1070, Spain) described the mystery of divine infinity in strict poetic meter. Philosopher Moses Maimonides (1135-1204, Spain and Egypt) crafted logical arguments about the Creator's infinity. Kabbalistic teacher Rabbi Israel Ba'al Shem Tov (1698-1760, Ukraine), a founder of the Hasidic movement, encouraged daily spiritual practice. If you are diligent, he said, the heavens may open and you may experience infinite consciousness. Obviously, I believe he is right. As you read on, I hope you will agree.

Opening to
Spiritual Traditions

✳

Recently, a new artisan storefront opened near my Main Street home. I like to support local artisans when I can. So, I wandered in for a look.

"Our name is Just Jewellery," said the salesperson. "We specialize in silver and semiprecious stones, featuring the work of several local artists…"

But I could not focus on her words. Instead, images of divinity overwhelmed me. I saw Ganesh, Hindu god of wisdom, carved in jade; Buddha, sculpted in a granite-like paste; a Kabbalistic network of triangles drawn with sparkles; a Cross embellished with garnet; a bold Eagle, etched in silver.

This store was a festival, but I was not sure what kind. A deeply multi-faith festival, celebrating devotional artistic intent? Or a superficial spiritual-not-religious marketplace, baiting buyers with aesthetic beauty?

"Please, take a closer look at something," the seller begged, "Even if you don't want to buy today!"

Focusing, I asked to see four pendants: a doubled *magen david* (Star of David); a flowing Sanskrit *Om*; St. Christopher carrying a child;

and a tree with roots in earth and heaven. The heavy garnet cross intrigued me, too; but I did not ask to see it. As a Jew, I could not imagine touching it.

Was this Christian symbol too sacred for me, or too terrifying?

Every Thursday, I attend community worship services at the Vancouver School of Theology, the Christian seminary where I work. And every Thursday, I ask myself a similar question.

I love our community worship. No two weeks are quite the same. Faculty sparkle; students experiment; everyone sings, whether they know the tune or not. We learn from one another about denominational worship styles, creative preaching, presence in leadership and more. Sometimes I participate, chanting Hebrew scripture or offering a Jewish prayer. No one minds that I never take communion and rarely say "Amen!"

"Amen" should be simple, but for me it is not. As the "Interfaith Amigos"—Pastor Don MacKenzie, Rabbi Ted Falcon, and Imam Jamal Rahman — say, the most challenging stage of the interfaith journey is "exploring spiritual practices from other traditions."

But should I not have reached that stage? That's my weekly question.

For forty years, I have gathered multi-faith knowledge, and pursued a spiritual formation beyond borders. Avoiding the superficial, I have earned degrees, diplomas and certificates from credible academic and professional programs. I have studied Western philosophy, Ayurvedic yoga, Kabbalistic Judaism, Christian spiritual direction, and Jungian depth psychology. And my studies have led me to an inclusive theology.

God is, as Christian Matthew Fox might say, the "one river" of spirit, bubbling up in "many wells" of tradition.

God is, in Kabbalistic Hebrew, *Eyn Sof*, Infinity. All human expressions of spirituality circle within the Infinite God. Every religious word, concept, sound, or ritual may turn us towards God, but cannot fully encompass the divine.

God is, as depth psychologists say, "psyche" —a totality of all possible experiences and influences. Psyche surrounds us, appearing to us as consciousness, while also directing us beyond consciousness.

God is, as I learned in yoga, *Brahman*, infinite energy, mirrored in *atman*, the individual soul.

Yet, when tested, my seamlessly inclusive theology begins to crack.

As it should! Because, as it admits, even this view of God is a partial representation. Unchallenged, it could harden into a kind of armour. Wearing it, I could fend off all new ideas. At best, new ideas would be pale reflections of what I already know. At worst, they would be childish and concrete compared with my grand vision.

So, when I attend community worship at the

The Infinity Inside

Vancouver School of Theology, I try not to wear my deep ecumenism as armour. Taking off the armour, though, leaves me vulnerable. Personal and collective memories of antisemitism bubble up. Then, I expect some monstrous person to leap up from their seat and accuse me of killing Jesus. And sometimes—even amid my euphoric enjoyment—I want to run from the room.

Of course, at thoughtful, engaged, and generous VST, no one accuses me. And I do not run from the room. Instead, I assume the posture of a good participant observer. I practice what Paul Ricoeur would call a "hermeneutic of recollection"—an expectation that I will collect meaning. I listen to the words, feel the music and watch people's movements. Spiritual energy fills the room. It stirs the participants' hearts to tears, euphoria, commitment to social justice, and a sense of peace. Their particular spiritual practice, I learn, awakens specific dimensions of their spirits. Dimensions I might not have known about, had I not stayed in the room.

A Walk in the Woods

✳

A day off. Wow. Did I even dare to pray for it? It's a rare treat in the religion business!

What to do? Where to go? My beloved and I chose Mt. Seymour, a provincial park just 30 minutes outside our city. Mountains, woods, rushing rivers. No cell phone service. No internet access. A different rhythm.

We parked at a high elevation and hiked down to the river gorge. The trail led us into dense, damp woods. Spanish moss, mushrooms, black slugs, nurse logs—under towering old growth pine and cedar trees. Deep quiet, woodsy smells, soft dark ground.

Our thoughts and feelings, too, became quiet and soft. As we hit the trail, we fantasized about breaking free of our frenetic life. We would create the family business of our dreams. But, under the spell of the woods, we gradually forgot all details of our everyday life. We talked only about what was before us. Leaf. Root. Rock. Creek.

Down in the gorge, the river ran fast and loud. We had no need to talk and couldn't hear one another if we did. At a pebble beach, we sat on boulders. We looked, we listened, we felt, we thought.

The Infinity Inside

From my pack, I took out a book of poetry by Solomon ibn Gabirol (1021-1058). We have no words, I thought, but surely this lover of infinity does. And he did have the perfect Hebrew words. So, I translated them:

> *Three hints together in a single view*
> *In this place, I am reminded of You.*
> *Under your skies I can recall Your name*
> *Forever they bear witness to Your fame.*
> *The place where I sit awakens my thought*
> *It's vast but not boundless like You, my Lord.*
> *My musings draw my attention inside*
> *My soul does bless You, always, Adonai.*

Here we were, amid those three things. Sky peeking through trees and opening up over the river. Earth so green and damp and fragrant. Thoughts so calm, flowing with the river. We weren't thinking of God, but we didn't need to. We had merged with the spirit of the place, feeling ourselves in the One world-soul, blessing Adonai by simply being.

We were praying, ibn Gabirol would say. But not with prayers found in a prayer book. Written prayers only offer concepts about God. Our prayer was deeper. More direct. We broke our mundane patterns of thought. We contemplated creation. We felt the spirit that pulses through it.

On our day off from the religion business, we encountered spirit.

Spiritual vs. Religious

✳

Obviously, at Mt. Seymour Charles and I had a spiritual experience.

Spirit is our experience of being alive. Our emotions, thoughts, beliefs, ideals, moods, attitudes, intuitions, sense of the sacred. Some events grab our attention and turn it towards spirit. We call those "spiritual experiences." Experiences that change our consciousness. Uplift us. Re-direct us. Inform us.

Our day on the mountain was a magical, grace-filled, day of higher consciousness -- but it was not spontaneous. It was the fruit of long-term spiritual practice. We sought out teachers, studied hiking, trekked regularly, and evolved our own style.

Years ago, I hiked with the AMC, American Mountain Club. From experienced teachers, I learned how to stay safe, use equipment, and respect the environment. I read books about ecology and the spirituality of place; took classes about sacred land with Indigenous teachers; studied stories about non-human animals in my own scriptural tradition. Charles took classes in earth science, studied orienteering, and learned how to backpack. Before every outing, he studied maps and trail guides, so he could feel the shape of each place. For fifteen years, we walked outdoors in some kind of park almost every weekend.

So, it's no wonder Mt. Seymour rewarded us with a mystical experience. We spent years developing a consciousness that attunes to our surroundings.

Would I call it a "religious experience"? I'm not sure I would. Here's a paraphrase of Emile Durkheim's famous sociological definition of religion:

A religion is a unified system of beliefs and practices about sacred things that unites people into one single community across time and space.

Charles and I practice a religion: Judaism. Our daily Jewish rituals around waking, eating, washing, and going to bed integrate the sacred into everyday life. Weekly practices set aside Shabbat as a special time for spiritual reflection. Seasonal practices give historical and spiritual meanings to the rhythm of nature. Interpersonal practices teach kindness, morality and social justice. Jews all over the world practice the basics in similar ways. We feel ourselves as a single, though diverse, Jewish community.

When Charles and I meditate down by the

Seymour River, we feel part of a world-wide bio-diverse community of creatures. Does this feeling help unite the Jewish people into a single community?

Judaism designates special days for tuning into the natural environment. *Tu BeShevat* is a day for celebrating and planting trees. *Sukkot* is a week of living outdoors, as our ancestors did in the wilderness. If Charles and I smelled the sweet damp forest on *Tu BeShevat* and flowed with the river on *Sukkot*, we would be in sync with the Jewish world. We would co-create Jewish community across time and space. We would be doing religion — as Durkheim sees it.

But if Charles and I only followed the Jewish ritual calendar, we would be spiritually poorer. We wouldn't have become familiar with ecological consciousness. Sought out scientific and Indigenous perspectives. Learned how to feel with other life forms. Come to seek and find the world-soul. And when the designated holidays came around, we couldn't teach about them in depth.

The day felt holy, but it was not religious. We stepped outside communal Jewish guidelines. Drew from multiple traditions to craft a personal discipline. Let go of mainstream Jewish language to describe our experience.

Yet the day boosted our religious knowledge. Our personal discipline gave us tools for Jewish practice. Showed us perspectives hidden by familiar religious language. Made it easier for us to live into the guidelines. Perhaps the day itself was "spiritual not religious." But the day's impact? That was spiritual *and* religious, too.

What is Spiritual Practice?

What do I mean by "spiritual practice?"
Spiritual means relating to spirit. *Practice* means doing something. *Spiritual practice* is the art of actively paying attention to your spirit.

Why do I call it an art rather than a science?
Scientific practice relies on clearly defined terms, uniform procedures for all practitioners, and objectively valid results. Spiritual practice explores ambiguous terms, through a variety of procedures, aiming at subjectively valid results.

What is spirit?
Spirit is an ambiguous term. Spirit can include your emotions, character, ideals, moods, motivations, attitudes, beliefs, sense of God.

Why pay attention to spirit?
Spirit expresses itself through our bodies, thoughts, feelings, actions, reactions, dreams and more. Its constant hum, and occasional explosions, inform everything we do. When we look at it directly, we gain insight and, gradually, mastery.

The Infinity Inside

What counts as practice?

Any ongoing, structured activity that shifts our attention to spirit. In my own life, I have written reflectively in journals, breathed deeply through hatha yoga postures, walked in beautiful outdoor places, read and re-read traditional poetic prayers, prayed through structured forms, analyzed metaphors in my dreams, sung along with devotional music, studied philosophy and Torah, drawn with crayons, sat in silence, set aside a Shabbat day, and talked directly with God.

Should we think of spiritual practice as a discipline?

Yes, if discipline means something like an academic discipline. As a beginner, you learn basic terms and activities. As you master them, you develop your own unique insight and style. No, if discipline means you punish yourself for skipping a session.

How does one learn a practice?

I have learned the basics from communities, teachers, and books. As a learner, I seek both experiential understanding and background knowledge. At times, I have simply encountered new practices; at other times, I have sought them out.

How does one choose a practice?

Some practices have been part of my life for decades. But I also add and subtract new practices every few months or years. When life events grab my attention, I choose a practice that can help me respond. For example, I may need to develop conscious body awareness and take up a walking practice; forgive more, and work with a forgiveness meditation; connect with my Jewish tradition and add a study practice. Research and consultation help me find the right practice.

Must spiritual practice be daily?

It should be regular, if you want to learn it well, practice it creatively, and use it to know your spirit. But the definition of regular depends on the practice, how well you know it, and on how your time is structured. Some regular practices aren't daily, e.g., praying for healing as you light Shabbat candles. Other regular practices, e.g., yoga, are done safely by beginners only when a teacher is present. Others, e.g., mindfulness meditation, require attention and quiet you might be able to arrange only twice a week.

Should one choose a practice that feels comfortable or challenging?

Both. Find an ongoing practice that uses activities you enjoy to focus on spirit. Enjoyment will entice you to return again and again. But when an urgent problem of spirit grabs your attention, know that exploration of it might challenge your ways of thinking and feeling.

Begin with Breath

✳

In *The Tree of Yoga,* B.K.S. Iyengar says: Don't confuse Hatha yoga with a passive healing modality like massage. Hatha yoga is active. He means: paying attention is the essence of yoga.

The yoga sutras of Patanjali define yoga as "stilling fluctuations of the mind." Yet Hatha Yoga Pradipika says it's all about "stilling the fluctuations of the breath." Both are accurate, says Iyengar. When you still the breath, you still the mind. You pay attention differently.

Try paying attention to the flow of your breath. To how your lungs feel as they expand. How your torso feels as the expanding lungs touch other tissues. And—how did you never notice this before—the way your legs seem to lengthen too. The breath actually fills your whole body.

Sure, you could get analytical and anatomical about the oxygenated blood filling your arteries. Or the diaphragm moving down and pushing other muscles with it. You might be suddenly curious about these processes.

But you file them away and keep attending to the breath. Because with every breath you feel more, you see more, you know more. You feel wonderful. Filled with quiet wonder.

The Infinity Inside

Some religious traditions will call this wonderful more by the name "God." The more you pay attention, the more you feel, see, and know God. Some teachers will add: you *must* refer this "more" to God, *must* pursue these experiences in service of God. Otherwise, your spiritual practice is selfish. You're only seeking to know more "you."

I disagree.

Please, *don't* rush to refer these experiences to an object called "God." The word "God" has meaning in a context. In relation to a theology, social order, philosophy of life, set of ritual practices. If you contextualize your experiences too quickly, you are only getting to know the context.

You may, of course, be trying to learn a context. Through first-hand experience, you better understand a spiritual vocabulary. You cultivate a particular kind of awareness. Bring to life a specific theology and philosophy. Learn new behaviours through ritual repetition. Find your place in a community's social order. Discover the "you" best suited to the context. It may be an excellent "you."

But if you are a seeker in search of the "more," you won't be satisfied. At some point, you'll need to be subversive. You'll look for a spiritual practice, ritual, or philosophy that redirects your attention. So that you can perceive "more."

This does not mean you are selfish. It may

mean you are humble, not ready to claim you know God through personal experience. Or that you don't define God experientially. Maybe you don't define God at all, or are skeptical of traditions that claim to.

Maybe your best path to "more" is open-ended...

Path of the
Labyrinth

✳

Walking the labyrinth is an ancient movement meditation. It is popular among Christians, but is probably much older than Christianity.

The practice is simple. With focus, you walk a winding path from margin to center, following a single route in and back out. The process invites spiritual metaphors, encouraging you to reframe your questions and quests.

You can read about it. But until you walk it, everything the books say may seem ridiculous. "It's a map of your spiritual life." "A microcosm of planet earth." "A cosmic map of creation." The claims get more and more grandiose.

So, just walk. See which metaphors come alive for you. Here are some that spoke to me, during different labyrinth walks.

My professional life is a labyrinth: As I entered the labyrinth, I posed a question about a professional dilemma. For months, I'd been wrestling anxiously with it. As I walked, I thought of all the crazy turns my work life has taken. None were ultimately wrong turns, but sometimes I wasted a lot of energy. As I walked, I felt irritated with myself, impatient with the world.

The Infinity Inside

I noticed an old-fashioned streetlamp standing oddly near the labyrinth. "What was the artist thinking?" I wondered. "Lighting the way of the pilgrim? How obvious can symbolism get?" Amused, I laughed out loud. The laugh was not a verbal answer to my question. But it felt good. After a laugh, the path back out from the centre felt easier; the familiar twists and turns felt expansive. Instead of anxiety around decisions, I felt gratitude for opportunities.

As I exited, I felt my labyrinth walk told a story of my life-cycle. When I was younger, I was wound tightly around my ambition. These days, I'd simply like to enjoy my work.

Creation is a labyrinth, and I mirror creation: Feeling whimsical, I challenged the labyrinth as I entered. "I would like to find myself! Show it to me!" As I walked, I noticed how well the labyrinth is set up for seeking. You enter and explore a quadrant in tight arcs. With a wide curl, you swing into another quadrant.

"This is exactly the path I've used to find myself over and over again," I thought. "Study a field carefully, leap into a new one, study it and leap again." But as I reached the center, I felt anxious; there's nowhere to leap. Should I stand still, or take tiny steps?

Stalled at the center, I surveyed the labyrinth: a big circle, filled with paths bending back upon themselves. Suddenly, I remembered a famous kabbalistic creation theory. Before the beginning, says the theory, only undifferentiated Divine energy existed. At some point, Divine energy contracted itself, leaving a circular void. A ray of divine light blazed through that circle, bending itself to create vessels to hold its own light. Some vessels shattered; others endured. All became part of the world we know.

In my own inner life, I realized, I recognize a void. An empty place, that can burn with intensity, holding feelings and fears. It propels me forward, to learn and explore. Learning never quenches it, only wraps around it, alternately hiding and fueling it. Yes, it hurts, but that's not a failing, it's just the way I am. It's the way of all creation, and I am a creature.

Planet earth is a labyrinth. One day, I brought my geeky self to the labyrinth on our university campus. I was determined to quantify and memorize the labyrinth's structure, quadrant by quadrant. So, as I walked, I counted. "Enter quadrant one, double back, walk circumference." "Enter quadrant two, circle round to three…"

Pausing in the count, I looked up.

To the north, I saw the castle, grey with faint patches of moss. East, the brown-bricked student residence. South, the glassy new white condominium tower. West, the matching lowrise apartments. And nestled within this quadrant of buildings: the lawn, the playground, the parking lot.

The Infinity Inside

My eyes circled the labyrinth closer in. I saw the tall straight pine, the deciduous grove, the old split sappy tree, and the garden of broadleaf greens.

My gaze wound back out. From the nearest circle of plants, to the larger circle of activity zones, to the campus building layout. This winding sweep mirrored the winding path of the labyrinth. Yes, I realized, anything can look like a labyrinth, a pattern, a journey, a path.

Welcome to the labyrinth, my surroundings said. Here's a metaphor that helps you reframe it all.

Chant

A Multi-faith Musical Language

Chanting is repetitive singing of a short phrase. The words are usually simple. Like: "Peacemaker, make peace." "Love your neighbor as yourself. " "All the world is holy." The tune can be simple, too. But interesting. Easy to learn. And fun to sing. (Assuming you like singing.)

To begin, you speak the words. Gradually, you learn the musical phrase. You begin to sing easily. You breathe rhythmically. Your body takes over, as the words and notes form themselves. You pay attention to the voices of others. Finally, a wave of feeling carries you into altered consciousness. New dimensions of spirit come forward.

That's the simple explanation. But Charles and I signed up for a workshop on multi-faith chant so we could go deeper. And of course we got tapped into leading the unit on Jewish chant. Here's what we learned at the workshop at Bethlehem Centre.

Chant is Holy Play: Trio SaySo—Allannah Dow, Leah Hokenson and Tina Jones—tossed us into the world of chant. We all have voice, they said. Sing out your names in introduction. You all can chant. Who among us hasn't sung "Hello kitty! Hello puppy!" Or "Coffee? Coffee!" Chant, they taught, can be spontaneous, playful and simple. It can be creative and varied. Why, they themselves had chanted both the love-murmurings of Rumi and the ecstatic shouts of Whitman!

Chant Shifts Our Awareness: Pandit Tejomaya placed chant in a Hindu context. Names of God are symbols for the one true divinity. We channel God through universal love. Spiritual practice removes barriers to that love. Tejomaya wove his teachings through trance-like Sanskrit chants. He played the sitar: one melodic string, amplified by the sympathetic drone of a dozen deeper strings. We vibrated with the sitar. Sanskrit words soothed us. Rich in rhythm, alliteration, meaning. The pace of our thoughts slowed. We opened to the teachings.

Chant Amplifies the Music of Speech: Chant, taught Christian choirmaster Peter Orme, amplifies the musical cadence of ordinary speech. The Bible was once oral tradition, spoken by poets. Later, great orators embellished its emotion. Choirs emphasized its rhythm and fine-tuned its tone. Gregorian Chant was born. Neither mysterious nor esoteric. But accessible, relevant, beautiful. Expressive of religious and artistic history. Let's bring it back, Peter said. And in no time flat, he taught us to read the charts and sing them into life.

Chant Helps Us Pray: Charles and I shared Hebrew chant as prayer. Where do you want the chant to take you? Opening to spirit? Letting go of negativity? Praying for healing? Channeling the breath of life? Listening deeply to others? Moving into ecstatic dance? Set an intention before you chant. As you lose yourself in the music, let the intention direct your attention. Trust your own spirit. Sometimes you can chant around a theme: Awe. Gratitude. Love. Or all three woven into a single spiritual cycle of receiving and giving. Connect with God in gratitude; find energy to help repair the world. That's the Jewish way.

Chant Connects Us in Community: Sufi teacher Seemi Ghazi came with musicians Amir and Ibrahim, dancers Raqib and Linda. Together they drew us, mind, body, and spirit into Sufi philosophy. God Is. One. Energy. Love. A spacious field of consciousness where we meet others. With a glance, we can hold them in love. And we did. We whirled around from partner to partner chanting. *All I ask of you is forever to remember me as loving you.*

My first partner pulled me close. "Those are the last words my daughter said to me before she died." We held hands tightly and cried together. Then we reached out. To partner after partner, we passed the Divine whisper. *Remember. I love you.*

Intuition

Opening the Heart

At the Ranger Station in Glacier, Washington, a slice of Douglas fir sits on a throne.

Near it, an interpretive sign says: *Growth rings spaced closely together indicate difficult growing periods, while rings spaced further apart indicate more prosperous seasons of development experienced by the tree.*

Oh, how I empathized! I've had difficult and prosperous times, too. Recalling them, I cried.

I reached out to the tree, touching its thick-ringed centre. Such a strong heart! I touched its burned part, too, at the narrow-ringed edge. "Lightning strike!" said the tree. "Fear, pain, much confusion, no explanation, and a slow healing process."

I kissed the narrowly spaced rings, then placed my palm at the fleshy heart. "Your momma loved you," I whispered, picturing a stand of fir. "You got a good start. You were birthed in blessing."

How did I know? How could I know if my perceptions were real or true?

At a local camping festival, someone asked my husband Charles that same question. Charles loves to tell people how I gather rocks for a particular type of Jewish memorial ceremony. After a formal gravestone is "unveiled," visitors place smaller, personal stones beside it. Each time Charles and I hike in a beautiful place, I stop to pick up pebbles. As I hold each pebble, I ask it, "Would you like to come on an adventure, and help people heal?" If the stone says, "yes," I put it in my pack. If it says "no," I thank it and return it to its place.

A friend at the festival asked: how does she know what the stone answers?

Charles doesn't really know how I know. But he loves to tell the story. Maybe because I used to teach logic and critical thinking. But more likely because he used to teach empirical psychology.

How *do* I know? The same way I know in any interpersonal interaction.

In any interaction, we touch and are touched by another — physically, emotionally, energetically. We receive sensations, feelings, images, ideas. We could call them subjective experiences. But it would be more accurate to call them "intersubjective." They come to us as the content of encounter. They are intersections, the connective tissue of the world.

How do I know? I hang out in the intersection.

I make myself really quiet and just listen. Turn off judgment, so I don't block important information with my own thoughts and feelings. Sometimes I don't know whose emotions I'm reading—mine or another's. But I don't worry, trusting that answers will come in time.

One day, while working as a synagogue rabbi at Or Shalom, I sat with four different people: one trying to rescue a relative lost in a foreign country, one who narrowly escaped danger alive, one making an uncertain career transition, and one hospitalized after a suicide attempt. Each one hoped for clarity, affirmation, and connection. But the only gift I had at hand to offer them was my presence. Was I afraid to be armed with such a limited tool? Yes. Was I afraid to have no prepared words, advice, or resources? Yes. So, I acknowledged the fear in a prayer addressed to God, understood the power of Presence.

Holy One, I am stepping into a situation about which I know nothing, and in which I may have nothing to offer. Help me be present, help me feel my feet on the ground, connected to the energy of Your earth. May Your energy flow through me, rising in my body, flowing out my hands, out the top of my head. May I be a channel who shares Your energy with others. May I be able to stand with them in Your Presence, as You guide us with your wisdom and your will.

Sometimes, as I led services on Shabbat, I would again play these words in my heart. Our service allowed me two opportunities to offer spontaneous words of prayer in English.

The Infinity Inside

So, over the years, I have spoken aloud, some 150 different prayers for peace and 150 different prayers for healing. These prayers are not prepared in advance. They emerge from the raw materials of congregational life and the content of that week's service or Torah reading. They are not preserved afterwards. As I return to ordinary consciousness, the details fade. If I could, I would collect the healing prayers into a book called *Fifty-Four Meditations: Healing Prayers for Each Torah Portion*. But I can't. The prayers do not form themselves when I sit in the presence of a text — only when I stand in the presence of people.

Praying with Beads

Examen of Conscience

"People from the United Church of Canada like to hug," said my colleague Brenda.

I filed this random fact away under *Important Information*. Little did I know it would soon come in handy.

A few days later, I received an email invitation: Might I facilitate a women's retreat for West Vancouver United Church? The women would love to learn with a woman rabbi.

Certainly, I said, and we set up a planning meeting. Three representatives from the Church would meet me at a local café.

As I walked through the door of the café, a man approached me. "Are you Laura?" he asked.

"I am!"

He gave me a light, friendly shoulder hug.

Well, I was a bit taken aback, but I remembered what Brenda said. So, I returned the hug and said, "I look forward to planning the retreat."

The man looked confused. "I was supposed to meet someone named Laura. We met over the Internet, and I don't know what she looks like."

"Well, my name is Laura, and I'm also supposed to connect with some people I met over the Internet. And I don't know what they look like either. ... But I don't think I'm your Laura."

Five minutes later, three women walked through the door. "Are you Laura?" they asked.

"I am!"

They each gave me a light, friendly shoulder hug.

On that familiar, funny basis, we began to plan a program, filled with Bible study, singing, dancing, crafts, study, prayer, and conversation.

One of the women, a skilled artist, had read a book called *A Bead and a Prayer: An Introduction to Protestant Prayer Beads,* by Kristen E. Vincent. Perhaps—she suggested—she could lead the women in making their own colorful prayer bead strands, and I could teach the group how to use them. She showed me a prototype: a circular string of 28 small beads, separated into groups of seven by four large beads. An even larger bead that she called a "resurrection bead" hung at one end, showing where to begin using the beads.

"Of course," I said. For these welcoming, affectionate women, I was willing to do anything! Even re-negotiate my interfaith borders and lead Christians in praying with beads.

Prayer beads are great concentration aids, especially for me. Sometimes I need help concentrating. With my keen hearing, sensitive skin, and motion-attuned vision, I constantly take in new information. And my mind always takes the bait, collating, cross-referencing, and interpreting what I perceive. But when I take up prayer beads, I close my eyes. I hold the beads, focusing on how they feel between my fingers. As my mind slows down, ordinary noises begin to sound more like music and less like information. Thus, my consciousness shifts.

At this retreat, I decided, I would use the beads to guide us through an *examen* or "examination of conscience." Inviting God as an inner witness, we would each take a private look at our own joys and worries. The *examen* is famous as a Catholic practice, but it appears in many spiritual traditions. The program organizers had specifically sought out a rabbi. So, I decided I would base the day's *examen* on four types of prayer, familiar to me from Jewish tradition: Praise *(shevach)*, confession *(vidui)*, intercession or petition *(bakashah)*, and gratitude *(hoda'ah)*. I would re-interpret the "resurrection" bead as a "life" bead, connecting us with the *chiyut*, energy, of God who is *chai ha'olamim* (life of all the worlds).

So I taught:

Hold the beads in your stronger hand, hanging them over your four fingers, with your thumb free to feel them. Let the bead of life rest in your hand. Feel its round shape, let associations to its meaning come to you.

The Infinity Inside

Find the rhythm of your own breath. With your thumb, feel the life bead as an invitation. As you breathe, affirm, "I am ready to move into prayer." As you touch the bead feel God's life in you and around you.

Touch the next big bead, the bead of praise, of awe and wonder. Which magnificent works of God are present to you today? As you move your fingers along the smaller beads, name seven moments of wonder; or take seven breaths; or simply feel seven beads and allow images to come to you.

Touch the bead of confession: inviting you to confess not just sins, but the big thoughts and feelings you carry with you today. With God as your inner witness, name the burdens you want God to see and help you carry. Seven burdens; or seven breaths; or seven beads.

Touch the bead of intercession. Intercede for yourself. Ask God to help you develop the inner qualities you need to live into your thoughts, feelings, and challenges. Seven qualities; or seven breaths; or seven beads.

Touch the bead of gratitude. Thank God for all you have received in the past, for all that gives you the faith to pray for help. Or thank God for all you expect to receive. Your prayers may not be answered in the way you imagined, but they will be answered. Seven expressions of gratitude; or seven breaths; or seven beads.

Return to the bead of life and feel God's life within you. Invite God to continue to be present to you, as you exit this time of reflection.

I created this *examen* particularly for this group. And I invite you to try it. I found it powerful; it continued to inspire me for months. Three times a week, I prayed in my own words, using a five-step process: acknowledging awe, confessing worries, seeking spiritual development, asking for healing, and offering gratitude.

One day, I prayed:

God, I am in awe of the mystery of consciousness, an amazing continuum in which creatures reach out, across space and across species. I confess, God, that I don't want to see the world through the veils of my own consciousness. And especially not through the lens of my own guilt, measuring my impact by how badly I feel. God, please grant me the ability to see differently. Please bring healing to political leaders so that they, too, no longer act out of their pain. Thank you, God, for this limited human body that structures my consciousness — until the day it merges with yours.

After trying this contemplative exercise, one of the women at the retreat said, "I feel as though God just gave me a big hug." (I am not making this up.)

Continuous Prayer,
Kabbalah Style

✳

Think about our Biblical ancestor Jacob. As a young man of about 19, he sets out to seek his fortune. On his first night away from home, he dreams. *A ladder connects earth and heaven; messengers climb up and down. Suddenly God stands right over him and speaks.* Jacob wakes suddenly from this numinous dream, infused with awareness of Divine presence. "God is in this place," he says, "and I, I did not know it!" He erects a monument.

Jacob thinks this is a dream about the place. *He does not understand that he himself is the ladder.* He is a conduit for Divine spirit. After years of joy and suffering, he will become a channel so strong that even the Pharaoh will ask for his blessing.

But, this morning, Jacob knows only his immediate mystical experience. He has no concepts to help interpret it. Like other characters in the Book of Genesis who walk and talk with God, Jacob simply accepts the spiritual magic of his world.

Over time, as Jewish literature documents, this acceptance faded. A thousand years later, the prophets, highly literate priests trained in the spiritual arts, spoke. They shared their visions, frustrated that others could neither see nor hear God's presence. A thousand years after that, rabbinic tradition began to teach that mystical experience is a secret. Do not write about it, teachers said, and speak of it only in private, with others who have hinted at similar experiences.

But numinous experiences continued to bubble up in public. By the year 1200, Jewish mystics were again writing and publishing their visions—most famously in the *Zohar*, literally "the shining book." The *Zohar* records dreams, visions, and imaginative journeys in free associative writing, loosely connected with Biblical text. It offers a theory of the nature of God to help explain how our psyche can channel Divine Presence: the theory of the *Sefirot*—accounts hinting at heaven.

Simply speaking, the *sefirot* are ten spiritual qualities: Emptying, Wisdom, Understanding, Love, Judgment, Balance, Endurance, Gratitude, Grounding and Presence. Less simply, the *sefirot* are attributes of God; qualities of human thought; energy centres of the body; spiritual blueprints for material creation; cosmic forces that sustain the world; metaphors for creativity and procreation—a multiplicity of ten mystically participating in a unity of One. Over the next 400 years, the theory grew more elaborate and complex.

In the late 1700s, Rabbi Israel Baal Shem Tov began to reverse the trend. Kabbalah, he taught, helps us regain a sense of God's mystical presence in everyday life. His early Hasidic movement experimented with practices we would call meditation, chanting, ecstatic dance and more. One simple practice, called by the Baal Shem Tov *hashgacha peratit,* God's attention to individuals, can be done anywhere, anytime.

Imagine it is a weekend morning, say, a Saturday at synagogue or a Sunday at church. You have resolved that this week, your participation will be meaningful. You are going to sing with passion, concentrate on the sermon, and pray sincerely for the healing of others. But, despite your intention, you find you cannot focus. You add items to your grocery list, worry about your sister, or resolve to join the local environmental protest despite your need for rest. Suddenly the service has ended; you have missed most of it; and you feel you have failed spiritually.

But don't worry, taught the Baal Shem Tov. You have *not* failed; you have actually soared spiritually. Each and every distracting thought has been a mystical visitation from God. A grocery list expresses your need for good judgment, structure and planning. The *sefirah* of Judgment has touched you. Worry for your sister shows your care, the *sefirah* of Love flowing through you. Your resolution to reach through exhaustion to repair the world is powered by the *sefirah* of Endurance.

You have had powerful mystical experiences through your everyday thoughts. Your psyche is a channel for God. Like Jacob, you may feel surprise. "God is in this place, and I, I did not know it!" You have climbed your own ladder.

Three Prayers a Day

A Jewish Examen

What if you are not so good at this continuous prayer? Let's say, you cannot remember the names of the *sefirot,* the spiritual qualities. Or you are simply too immersed in events of the day to catch every spiritual cue. Thus, you need to set aside a few specific, structured moments for prayerful reflection. The Jewish tradition of praying three times a day can be helpful.

If you are new to this practice, you don't have to start by studying all the words in the *Siddur* (prayer book). You can simply begin by noting three spiritual stations of the day. Begin the morning with gratitude; gather your strength in the afternoon; hope for forgiveness and protection in the evening. In a sense, this is an *examen of conscience* that threads throughout the day.

You may know that, according to the Bible, days begin in the evening. "It was evening, it was morning, one day" says Genesis 1:5. Our holiday cycle follows this pattern. Holidays begin at sunset, and end at dark on the following day. But the daily spiritual practice calendar is different. Our traditions of daily spiritual practice follow the rhythm of human life.

The Infinity Inside

We wake in the morning, ideally after a good sleep, feeling refreshed. The new day has so much potential, we think. There's so much to be grateful for. We are alive, awake, thinking, and feeling. Early morning is a good time to make a list of things you are grateful for. You can write it in bed, sing it in the shower, or just think it as you commute to work. If you're not sure how to begin, the *Siddur*'s morning service offers a few suggestions. Begin with the phrase *modeh ani:* I am grateful in your presence, living and eternal spirit.

Continue by enumerating what you are grateful for. Draw on the list of Morning Blessings set out in the *Siddur;* go beyond it, if you are so moved. "We are grateful to you, God," says the *Siddur*, "You give the rooster (or the alarm clock) wisdom to discern day from night. You created me in your image. You give sight to the blind, and insight to the confused. You clothe the naked. Free prisoners. Straighten the bowed. Stretch out the earth over the waters. Satisfy my needs. Make my steps firm. Gird me with strength. Crown me with splendor. Give me strength when I am weary."

By afternoon, we may be tired. Or in the midst of solving knotty problems. We may be discouraged — or elated. If we are working, or parenting, we may have many active hours ahead. Thus, it's helpful to pause in the afternoon for a quick spiritual self-assessment. The *siddur's* afternoon psalm (145), which praises what God offers human beings, offers some suggestions. About what do I feel strong? Where do I need emotional support? Physical healing? Have I been compassionate? Can a deeper awareness of my spirit help me? I like to follow the assessment with a deep breath and a simple whispered formula. "Holy one, Inner witness, Power greater than myself: help me hold it all."

By nightfall, the day may weigh heavily on us. We may have received catastrophic news. Or just made some mistakes we need to correct. Some interactions may have been were awkward. Maybe we had a great day. But now we are tired. What seemed like great news a few hours ago doesn't seem so good anymore. Our elation led us to generate long to do lists that we'll never complete. Someone is to blame, but we're not sure who. Sure, we could take all the worries with us to bed, hoping that sleep alone will heal them. But sleep might not come, or, if it does, it might bring bad dreams.

It's helpful to let go of the day's troubles. You could sit or lie down quietly and breathe. Think of someone or something who has upset you today. Then, let the thought go. Visualize an awkward interaction. Replay it once in your imagination. Then, let the image go. Think of a relationship you'd like to heal. In your imagination, let the person know your desire. Then, let go of that big responsibility. And then, remind yourself: letting go is a step towards forgiving. Not towards forgetting, but towards lessening the pain you carry. Then, feel into, think, or recite these words, adapted from the traditional bedtime forgiveness meditation:

Master of the Universe: I hereby forgive anyone who has angered or who has upset me, or has done me any harm; who has harmed my physical body, my possessions, my honor; anything pertaining to me; whether accidentally or intentionally, by speech or by deed, in this incarnation or any other; any human being. And may no one be punished on my account. May it be Your will, my God, and God of my ancestors, that I continually walk upon the path of holiness and that I do not lapse into unconsciousness or indifference. May I receive the power to transmute past unconscious thoughts, words, and deeds into radiant awareness and loving right action.

(Version by Rabbi David Zaslow)

You can choose to close by asking for protection as you forgive. The *Siddur* suggests two ways to do so. You can draw on the bedtime service and ask for angelic protection:

May I be accompanied by the angels Michael, Gabriel, Uriel, and Raphael, agents of uniqueness, strength, light, and healing.

Or you can follow the evening service and ask God directly:

Spread over me your shelter of peace; turn away violence, hunger, suffering, and temptation; guard me as I come and go; bring me renewed life in the morning.

Try it. Not just for a day. But for a week, or a month. Begin the day with gratitude and end it with forgiveness. It might just be the spiritual ladder you need.

Journey into
Formal Liturgy

Shacharit

Let's say you've explored these three spiritual stations. You've relied on your imagination, your own relationship with God and spirit, and a few hints from the *siddur*. Now you are ready to go deeper, to work with the poetic and liturgical tools that fill the *siddur*.

Or, more likely, you have used the *siddur*. You know that the word *siddur* means order, the order of prayer. You may even be familiar with key prayers. You know that some are biblical excerpts and others are poems. But you are not sure what order the *siddur* follows. What logic, you wonder, informs the order of prayer? The liturgy, you know, expresses a theology — a theory about God. How does it stimulate inner *spirituality* — an encounter with God?

Here is an introduction to the morning service, meant to begin to answer those questions. This introduction shows how a single liturgy traces a particular spiritual journey. It relies on the fullest version of the service, the one the *siddur* recommends for Torah reading days: Mondays, Thursdays, Shabbat and holidays.

Pesukei D'Zimra (Verses of Song). Morning services begin with Psalms. Singing psalms together lifts us up over the synagogue threshold. With rhythmic breath, we engage our bodies. With dramatic music, we stimulate our emotions. We conclude with Psalm 150, honouring the spirit—if not the actual intent—of the great 1st century Rabbi Yossi the Galilean who said, "May I be among those who complete the book of psalms every day."

Shema and Its Blessings. With bodies and emotions engaged in praise, we focus our thoughts, first through theology and then through contemplation. Theologically, we reflect on monotheism. As the great medieval philosopher Moses Maimonides said, "What does it mean for God to be One? God is not *one* like a genus which subsumes many species, nor *one* like a body divisible into parts, nor *one* like the first in a series. To understand this is a positive commandment, for it is written in Deuteronomy: *Shema Israel: Listen Israel, The LORD our God, the LORD is ONE.*"

Amidah. Dwelling in the mystery of the ONE brings us into contemplative intimacy with God. During the *Kedushah*, or holiness prayer, we place ourselves right into Isaiah and Ezekiel's visions of heaven. The *Kedushah* is part of a practice we call *Amidah*, standing in the presence; or *Tefillah*, deepest prayer; or *Shemoneh Esrei*, eighteen blessings. Quietly, we reflect on eighteen issues of personal and communal concern. Our modern prayer book offers a poetic script to guide the reflection, but the sages who created the practice thought each person should reflect on the issues in their own way.

Torah Service. With our hearts and minds opened to Divine presence, we listen for God's speech. Our sages say that "*Torah* was written with black fire on white fire." Black fire refers to the letters; white fire to the spaces between them. When a reader chants from a first-century style *Torah* scroll, pronouncing the words, and pausing in the spaces, we are each touched differently. With songs and blessings, we celebrate the power of the reading.

Closing. Our closing hymn is usually a grand medieval poem that bridges heart and mind, earth and heaven, or time and eternity. *Adon Olam*, Master of Time and Space, describing an experience of God both transcendent and immanent, is a favorite for Shabbat morning. Its meter marks time so perfectly, that it can be sung to almost any tune, and brought to life in almost any emotional key.

Transitions. In between each section of the service, we usually chant the Aramaic **Kaddish,** sanctification prayer, composed around the year 600. The *Kaddish* encourages us to climb a ladder of spiritual engagement, helping us declare with each step, "Let's raise up God's name higher than any blessing, poem, praise or petition ever recited in this world! And let's all say Amen!"

Blessing in Action

✳

The *siddur* overwhelms us with images of God. God is felt in our breath and movement. God is felt in music and poetry. God is beyond number, beyond words, beyond infinity. And yet. Most often it calls God "King." As in *Blessed are You, Adonai our God, King of the universe.* If we love democracy, why idealize an autocrat? Is "king" a good metaphor for God? I wonder about this almost every day.

First thing in the morning, I like to take a 3-block walk to the Grind Café and Gallery on Main Street. Once I'm there, I like to sit near the window and watch the street before it's fully woken up. There's a little patch of sky I can see, right over Locus restaurant, and its color forecasts the day: blue or grey.

If I'm lucky, I get fifteen quiet minutes to read and write and reflect and, sometimes, to cry. The Grind is a kind of chapel for me. It's like a *schule*, a synagogue, because it's a neighborhood. It's a microcosm, which means, a little universe. And a lot of prayer happens there.

There's the quiet man who comes every day with two parrots, one on each shoulder; the toddler who shrieks with delight at each passing truck; the Friday Men's Torah study in the back;

and the owners, Michelle and Jay, who make every customer feel welcomed and honored.

There is the older gentleman who used to sit outside with his very shy dog. When I didn't see either of them for many months, I wondered whether the bad weather kept them home. Finally, one day the man came in alone and I asked him, "How is your dog?" Tears exploded from his face, and all he could choke out was, "It was horrible." And all I could say was, "You must really miss her."

One day, we—that is, the Grind morning community—noticed a commotion across the street in front of Locus restaurant. Three dogs and four people seemed agitated. We figured out that one of the dogs had bitten one of the people. But before any of us could cross the street to help, a very dignified man with a very dignified golden retriever had appeared. They took charge of the situation. The man spoke with each of the people. The golden retriever spoke with each of the dogs. (I am not making this up.) Then the man and the golden retriever escorted the injured woman and her Chihuahua home. They appeared; they helped; they left, like messengers from a higher order.

And it happened in front of Locus restaurant. "Locus" is Latin for "the place." This is the place. This is the microcosm. If God is King, this is the Kingdom. And this is where I come to pray.

God's Kingdom: this is an easy metaphor to wrap our minds around. God's Kingdom, where we are all citizens. We all pay our taxes, and we all receive our benefits. But the government allocations are not always fair. So, the private sector, you and me, have to pick up the slack. We reach across communication differences; we comfort the bereaved; we take charge when others are confused.

But our *siddur* doesn't just talk about God's kingdom. It talks about God as King. And this is a more difficult metaphor.

A metaphor compares two things that not really alike. So, when we meet a strange metaphor, we pause and think about the two things that are compared. In the process, we may learn about both things.

Our usual approach would be to try to think about the ways in which the two things are alike. So, we might ask: How is God like a King?

But, say our sages, this approach is backwards.

When we call God "King," we are declaring that we owe allegiance to NO earthly king. That we are subjects of the King who is NOT a king. That our highest principle is different from what any earthly king represents. So, when call God "King," we are supposed to think about how God is NOT like a king.

When you go about this way, the metaphor seems pretty obvious to me.

The Infinity Inside

When I picture a king, I picture a richly dressed person, sitting on a throne. When I picture God, I picture a buzzing energy that animates everything.

A king amasses material wealth. God's energy extends throughout the world, so God doesn't need any wealth.

A king competes with peers. God has no peers. Nothing has ever overridden the human quest to reach for spiritual meaning.

You can influence a king by sending aristocrats in the king's court to negotiate for you. But with God, as our sages teach, *rachamana liba b'ai*, God desires the heart. With God, communication is heart to heart.

When I call God "King," I mean that a divine energy uniting all life fills the world and calls my deepest heart of hearts to reach out. I pledge to discover the richness in this heart, and to bring those riches to daily life in the kingdom. I make this pledge knowing that, as I look into my heart, I may not discover what I expect. My own actions might surprise me.

Contemplating
Scripture

✳

The Shema

Shema! Listen!

It's the first word of the most famous sentence in Jewish liturgy.

Shema Yisrael, HaShem Eloheinu, HaShem Echad

According to the Torah, Moses speaks these words to the Israelites shortly before his death (Deut. 6:4). I won't be your spiritual guide anymore, Moses says. Spiritual practice is up to you. So, listen up!

Here's the best-known English translation:

Listen Israel, the LORD our God, the LORD is One.

And here's an English translation that captures more nuances of the Hebrew.

Listen you who wrestle with God! Remember, Moses hints, that our ancestor Jacob wrestled just before he received his spiritual name Israel.

The Ineffable Infinite Being, the Breath-of-life. Here Moses specifically uses the "tetragrammaton," the four letter-name of God. It's a variation on the word "being." We don't know how to pronounce it. But if we try, we make the sound of a breath.

The Infinity Inside

Is revealed to us through creation. Moses calls God "our Elohim." The book of Genesis speaks of "Elohim" creating our world. "Elohim" names the aspects of God revealed to us through our life in the world.

The Ineffable Infinite Breath of Life is One. A puzzle, as the medieval philosopher Maimonides later explained, beyond the reach of our cognitive minds. You'll have to wrestle with this one, says Moses, through your own spiritual practice.

And then, using exactly 42 Hebrew words, Moses gives some suggestions for spiritual practice. Everyone: love God with all your heart, soul, and might. Activists: express love in your thoughts and deeds. Contemplatives: use the words I just spoke as a mantra, a guiding phrase in your heart. Use it in sitting meditation and walking meditation; you can lie on the floor, too. Busy people: grab a moment to meditate in the quiet moments just before sleep and just after waking. Teachers: be creative and invent fun ways to teach the mantra to children. Artists: write it into amulets to decorate arms and foreheads. Builders: incorporate it into the design of homes. Travellers: ground yourself with it each time you pass through a gate. *(This is a creative reading of Deuteronomy 6:5-9.)*

Forty-two words bring God close, to invoke God. You might say: forty-two words to name God. In fact, rabbinic tradition teaches that, when the Jerusalem Temple stood, the High Priest knew several secret names for God. Once a year, the priest would enter a restricted room, the Holy of Holies. There, he would pronounce the forty-two-letter name to invoke God's presence. "Through your name," he would say, "help us atone for our sins." Let this invocation of you begin our process of contemplation and change.

Traditions of the High Priest are lost to us today. But traditions of invoking God in forty-two sounds continue in Jewish spiritual practice. The Baal Shem Tov taught students to make special use of prayer formulas of forty-two words. One is Moses' speech, which Jews call *v'ahavta*, "you shall love." We should say these words, the Baal Shem Tov taught, in a particularly slow and meditative way. Seven seconds per word.

How do you devote seven seconds to each word? So that it takes a full five minutes to read forty-two words aloud? Two different ways come to my mind.

One meditative method uses a breathing technique. Take a deep breath in. As you say the first word slowly, breathe out. Draw the sound out for the full length of your breath. Pause. Allow your body to absorb the oxygen, so you don't hyperventilate. Then, take another deep breath in. Breathe out the second word. And so on.

As B.K.S. Iyengar writes in *The Tree of Yoga*: "The mind can go in many directions in a split second. But the breath cannot go in many directions at once. It has only one path: inhalation and exhalation. Controlling the breath and observing its rhythm bring the consciousness to stillness." When your consciousness quiets down, it unclutters. Judgments and interpretations begin to fall away. Breath reveals a purer kind of being. Something ineffable.

The second meditative method is listening technique. Say the first word. Pause. Feel into the meaning of the word. Wait in silence for a few seconds. Say the next word. Focus on it alone; feel its meaning; wait. Do it again for each of the forty-two words. Allow familiar words to sound new and strange to you. This is a mode of wonder, similar to what Abraham Joshua Heschel called "radical amazement." When we perceive with wonder, he says in *God in Search of Man*, we allow God's glory to shine through. We also develop intuition, the ability to wait, listen, and receive. To hang out at the intersections. And to feel others' desires for connection – even when the right words are missing.

Making it Your Own

Revisiting the Shema

Shema. Listen.

Listen to your own intuition, creativity, spiritual style. We are not required only to follow practices invented by other teachers.

So, one day, I listened to my own body as it breathed. More carefully than usual.

First, I did some early morning *Hatha Yoga.* Sun salutations, triangle side bends, spinal twists. *Pranayama,* the breath of life.

Then, I sat down right where I was and whispered the morning *Shema* and *v'ahavta.*

In rhythm with my breath. Spontaneously, that's how it sorted itself out.

Seven phrases, seven breaths.

Each time I breathed in, I reflected on a phrase.

Some phrases name a part of the body. So, for those, I felt my breath touch the body part. Expand it, stretch it, emphasize it. Keep its *chakra* (wheel of energy) spinning.

Other phrases talk about Spirit, about God. So, for those, I simply breathed and let Spirit fill me. Yes, Hebrew sometimes uses the same word for breath and spirit. *Ruakh.*

The Infinity Inside

Then, after breathing a phrase in, I paused. With an expectant mind.

And, finally, I breathed out slowly. With a quiet, listening mind.

Then, I waited for the next phrase. It would tell me how to breathe. And the breath would tell me how to pay attention.

Here's how the seven phrases, seven breaths sorted themselves out:

(1) **Shema Yisrael, Adonai Eloheinu, Adonai Ekhad.** "Listen, Israel, Adonai is our God, Adonai is One." Shema—listen to the breath.

(2) **Barukh Shem Kivod Malkhuto l'olam va'ed.** "Blessed be the Name of the Glorious Kingdom forever and ever." Let the breath fill the body with glory.

(3) **V'ahavta et Adonai Elohekha bekhol livavkha u'v'khol nafshekha u'vekhol me'odekha.** "Love God with all your heart, all your soul, and with all your might." Breathe into your heart, throat, and third eye [between the eyebrows] *chakras*.

(4) **V'hayu hadevarim haeyleh asher anokhi mitzavkha hayom al levavekha, v'shinantam l'vanekha v'dibarta bam.** "Let these things that I instruct you today be on

98

your heart, teach them to your children, and speak of them." Again, breathe into your heart, throat, and third eye *chakras*.

(5) *B'shivtekha biveitekha u'vlekhtekha baderekh u'vshokhbekha u'vekumekha.* "As you sit at home, walk on your way, lie down, and wake up." Breathe into your root [base of spine] *chakra*, into your entire spine, and up towards your third eye.

(6) *U'keshartam li'ot al yadekha, v'hayu litotafot beyn eyenekha.* "Tie them as a sign onto your hands; let them be amulets between your eyes." Breathe from the root into your spine again. Allow breath to flow down your arms to your fingertips, and flow up to your third eye.

(7) *U'khtavtam al mezuzot beitekha u'vi'she'areikha.* "Write them on the doorposts of your home and on your gates." Breathe into your whole body, to the crown [top of head] *chakra* and beyond, because your whole body has become a gate.

You can try this, too. And feel into it. Your body, full of oxygen. Full of energy, *ruach*, spirit. Vibrating. Attentive. Awake. Unified. Your body, with a message about spiritual living. *As you sit, as you walk, as you lie down to end a day, your heart fills. You teach, you speak, your eye awak-*

The Infinity Inside

ens. Your gate opens. Your hands extend. You live, you learn, you teach, you grow, you act.

One Finger Pointing

Pointing

✳

Charles and I found ourselves on the delta at Boundary Bay. Our quest to see snowy owls was successful.

The owls have flown south for winter. The Fraser River Delta looks arctic enough for a stop. It offers wide open water, a snowy mountain background, and short grasses alive with tasty rodents.

To the owls, our delta is a winter luncheonette. But to us, an exotic white owl is a gift of grace. Each owl sighting brings together photographers, bird watchers, naturalists, outdoor tourists, and spiritual seekers. We stand, silent and motionless as a perched owl, worshipping from a respectful distance.

Behind the snowy owl sits snowy Mt. Baker. If the owl is like a gift of grace, Mt. Baker is like a god. Massive, established, ancient, volcanic. Always visible, always hidden. Stable yet filled with mysterious inner dynamics.

Mt. Baker is only 11,000 feet tall. Compared to the sapphire blue sky, Mt. Baker is an infinitesimal micron. Mt. Baker's cone is only 90,000 years old. Compared to a creator said to sit on the sapphire throne, Mt. Baker is a fleeting twinkle in someone's eye.

Imagine a god conceived to be so ancient that it shatters the definition of "ancient." Or so big that "big" isn't even a relevant category. All you can say is: this God is "eternal" and "infinite." The words are cold and abstract. It's easier to glimpse infinity by silently scanning for owl, mountain and sky. No wonder the philosopher Maimonides speaks of "negative theology." Words can only say what God is *not*.

Jewish tradition is filled with words about God. Words so beautiful and challenging, they seduce us into positive theology. We take the words too seriously, imagining they pinpoint God's nature. And then, frustration trips us up. The words can't express the wild energy we touch. And God doesn't do what the words promise.

One Shabbat at Or Shalom Synagogue we gathered for a group study session about prayer. Our leaders John and Gloria placed before us a famous liturgical poem, the *Gevurot* (Powers) section of the *Amidah*. We read:

You sustain the living with loving-kindness, and with great compassion revive the dead. You support the fallen, heal the sick, set captives free, and keep faith with those who sleep in the dust.

One member of our group asked, "Are we supposed to take this as literally true?" Because if you read these lines as a theological statement, they are false, she said. God does not do these things with consistency. God certainly did not heal my two late husbands.

But if you read the lines as a prayer, said our leaders, they are true. That is, they express a yearning. Many of us long for a Supreme Being, World Controller, Source of Inner Power who will consistently support, heal, and free us.

The *Gevurot* is a masterpiece of negative theology. It does not tell us who God is. It only reminds us how we point towards God.

The religion of Judaism is like one finger pointing at the moon. But once you've seen the moon, what is the finger?

Once the practices have changed your perception, how does your perception of the practices change?

Once you've seen the owl, the volcano, and the sapphire sky, where do you look next?

To Infinity and Beyond

✳

Adon Olam

Solomon Ibn Gabirol
A Jew raised in Muslim Spain
11th century

Known to Jews
as a literary artist
a liturgical poet
of wild imagination and skill

Known to Muslims
as a philosopher
in the Neo-Platonic tradition
able to put the subtlest metaphysical intuitions
into a single word

Solomon Ibn Gabirol
Likely the author of *Adon Olam*

You know *Adon Olam*,
The last song
of the Shabbat morning service

The Infinity Inside

Adon Olam Asher Malach
B'terem kol yetzir nivra

Adon Olam Asher Malach
B'terem kol yetzir nivra

And you know its *peshat*
Its simple translation

Master of the World Who Ruled
Before every thing was created

Master of the World Who Ruled
Before every thing was created

But Ibn Gabirol
poet and philosopher
was not thinking *peshat*
was not thinking simple

He was thinking deep
Adon Olam Asher Malach

Adon
From biblical Hebrew
Adanim
Joints
The matrix that holds a structure together

Olam
Eternal in time
Infinite in space
Elusive
Hidden

Adon Olam
The Hidden Matrix that holds reality together

Asher
Not just a preposition
But an adjective
Happy, joyous, blissful

Adon Olam Asher
If you grasp this matrix,
you feel joy
and bliss
your most sublime moments of peace
radiate
in every direction

The Infinity Inside

Malach
From the word *malchut*
royalty
In Kabbalah
a synonym
for *Shechinah*
The one who dwells
The indwelling presence
Dwelling every where
In every thing

Adon Olam Asher Malach
The indwelling elusive matrix of bliss

B'terem kol yetzir nivrah

B'terem
Before
in the before
in the great before

Kol Yetzir
Everything that has form

Nivra
was created

B'terem kol yetzir nivra
Before anything with physical shape
Anything with conceptual form
or boundaries
of any kind
was created

Before even a thought
of creation
Before a design
or a plan
arose

The indwelling
elusive matrix of bliss
existed

But "existed"
is a verb
in the past tense form
And until beings
with form
were created
There was no
past tense
There was no
"before"

The Infinity Inside

Only
an indwelling
elusive
matrix of bliss

There was no
infinity
Because infinite
means
"not finite"
And without finite beings
Who can measure
infinity?

Oh Infinity!
A poor concept
Product
of the short reach
of the human mind
as it tries
to grasp
the elusive
indwelling
matrix of bliss

Infinity!
A marvelous angel
God's first
created concept
Our very best tool
To touch
The matrix
Of bliss

Infinity
a measure
a hint
The footsteps of time

Marked out
by the poet
In his rhythmic words

Adon Olam Asher Malach
B'Terem Kol Yetzir Nivra

When I,
Laura,
Pray

The Infinity Inside

I often ask:
Holy One,
help me
hold it all,
all my thoughts,
all my feelings,
all my fears,
all my failures
Because you,
Holy One,
already hold them
in your elusive matrix

B'yado afkid ruchi
Into this cosmic hand
I assign
my spirit
Trusting
it is held
in the matrix

B'eit Ishan
When it's time for sleep
I
whose bodily life
is timed
down to the minute
By hormones, neurons, and nutrients
Conforming to a circadian rhythm
Living 16 of 24 hours
at full attention

I
surrender my control
for 8 hours
I let
the matrix
hold me

V'a'iyra
Until I wake up
and beyond

V'im ruchi geviyati
With my soul expressed
through this time-bound form

The Infinity Inside

Adonai Li
My concept
of an infinite God
keeps me company

V'lo Irah
Irah, to see
Irah, to fear

Though I will never see
the matrix
itself
It holds me
I will not fear

Bibliography

Abram, David. *The Spell of the Sensuous.* New York: Vintage Books, 1997.

Abrams, Judith Z. *The Other Talmud: The Yerushalmi: Unlocking the Secrets of The Talmud of Israel for Judaism Today.* Woodstock, VT: Jewish Lights, 2012.

Artress, Lauren. *Walking a Sacred Path: Rediscovering the Labyrinth as a Spiritual Practice.* New York: Penguin, 1995.

Ba'al Shem Tov, Rabbi Israel. *Tzavaat HaRivash: Testament of Rabbi Israel Baal Shem Tov.* Translated and annotated by Jacob Immanuel Shochet. Brooklyn, New York: Kehot, 1998.

Bisson, Christian A., and Jamie Hannon. *AMC's Mountain Skills Manual: The Essential Hiking and Backpacking Guide.* Boston: Appalachian Mountain Club, 2017.

Bourgeault, Cynthia. *Centering Prayer and Inner Awakening*. Plymouth UK: Cowley Publications, 2004.

Durkheim, Emile. *The Elementary Forms of Religious Life*. Oxford University Press, 2001.

Falcon, Ted, and David Blatner. *Judaism for Dummies*. Hoboken, New Jersey: John Wiley and Sons, 2001.

Fox, Matthew. *One River, Many Wells: Wisdom Springing from Global Faiths*. New York: Tarcher/ Penguin, 2000.

Green, Arthur, and Barry Holtz. *Your Word is Fire: The Hassidic Masters on Contemplative Prayer*. Jewish Lights, 1993.

Hammer, Reuven. *Entering Jewish Prayer: A Guide to Personal Devotion and the Worship Service*. New York: Schocken Books, 1994.

Halbertal, Moshe. *Maimonides: Life and Thought*. Princeton: Princeton University Press, 2015.

Heschel, Abraham Joshua. *God in Search of Man: A Philosophy of Judaism*. Farrar, Straus and Giroux, 1976.

Hillman, James. *Revisioning Psychology*. San Francisco, CA: Harper, 1975.

Ibn Gabirol, Solomon. *The Fountain of Life (Fons Vitae)*. Ashland, OH: Baker & Taylor Library of Alexandria, 2009.

Ibn Gabirol, Solomon. *Selected Religious Poems of Solomon Ibn Gabirol.* Translated by Israel Zangwill. Philadelphia: Jewish Publication Society, 1944.

Ibn Gabirol, Solomon. *Vulture in a Cage: Poems by Solomon ibn Gabirol.* Translated by Raymond P. Scheindlin. Brooklyn NY: Archipelago, 2016.

Isherwood, Christopher, and Swami Prabhavananda. *How to Know God: The Yoga Aphorisms of Patanjali.* Vedanta Press, 1953.

Iyengar, B.K.S. *The Tree of Yoga.* Boston: Shambhala Press, 1989.

Jung, Carl Gustav. *On the Nature of the Psyche.* Translated by R.F.C. Hull. Princeton, NJ: Princeton University Press, 1960.

Kaplan, Laura Duhan. "Body, Mind, and Breath: A Mystical Perspective." In *Philosophy and Everyday Life,* edited by Laura Duhan Kaplan, 231-238. New York: Seven Bridges Press, 2001.

Kitov, Eliyahu. *The Book of Our Heritage: The Jewish Year and Its Days of Significance.* Nanuet, NY: Feldheim Publishers, 1978.

Lad, Vasant. *Strands of Eternity: A Compilation of Mystical Poetry and Discourses.* Albuquerque, NM: The Ayurvedic Press, 2004.

Leaman, Oliver. *Jewish Thought: An Introduction.* New York: Routledge, 2006.

Mackenzie, Pastor Don, Rabbi Ted Falcon, and Imam Jamal Rahman. *Getting to the Heart of Interfaith: The Eye-Opening, Hope-Filled Friendship of a Pastor, a Rabbi & an Imam.* Woodstock, VT: Skylight Paths, 2009.

Maimonides, Moses. *The Guide for the Perplexed.* Translated by M. Friedlander. Mineola, NY: Dover Publications, 1956.

Maimonides, Moses. *Sefer Hamada, Book of Knowledge.* Edited by Rabbi Eliyahu Touger. New York: Moznaim, 2010.

Prager, Marcia. *The Path of Blessing.* Woodstock, VT: Jewish Lights Publishing, 2003.

Rahman, Jamal. *Spiritual Gems of Islam: Insights & Practices from the Qur'an, Hadith, Rumi & Muslim Teaching Stories to Enlighten the Heart & Mind.* Woodstock VT: Skylight Paths, 2013.

Rainbow Spirit Elders. *Rainbow Spirit Theology: Towards an Australian Aboriginal Theology.* Adelaide, Australia: ATF Press, 2008.

Ricoeur, Paul. *Freud and Philosophy: An Essay on Interpretation.* Translated by D. Savage. New Haven, CT: Yale University Press, 1970.

Schachter-Shalomi, Zalman. *Jewish With Feeling.* Woodstock, VT: Jewish Lights Publishing, 2013.

Scholem, Gershom. *Major Trends in Jewish Mysticism.* New York, NY: Schocken Books, 1995. (Original work published in 1946)

Shankara, "The Crest-Jewel of Discrimination." In *Voices of Wisdom: A Multicultural Philosophy Reader,* edited by Gary E. Kessler. Belmont, CA: Wadsworth, 2015.

Thibodeaux, Father Mark E. *Reimagining the Ignatian Examen: Fresh Ways to Pray from Your Day.* Chicago: Loyola Press, 2015.

Tishby, Isaiah. *Wisdom of the Zohar.* Translated by D. Goldstein. Washington, DC: Littman Library of Jewish Civilization, 1989.

Ulanov, Ann, and Barry Ulanov. *Primary Speech: A Psychology of Prayer.* Louisville, KY: Westminster John Knox Press, 1982.

Vincent, Kristen E. *A Bead and a Prayer: A Beginner's Guide to Protestant Prayer Beads.* Nashville, TN: Upper Room Books, 2013.

Wolfe-Blank, Rabbi David. *Meta Siddur: A Jewish Soul-Development Workbook.* Kensington, CA: David Wolfe-Blank, 1995.

Woodley, Randy. *Shalom and the Community of Creation: An Indigenous Vision.* Grand Rapids, MI: Eerdmans, 2012.

Steinsaltz, Adin. *The Thirteen-Petalled Rose.* New York: Basic Books, 2006.

Zaslow, Rabbi David. *Ivdu et Hashem b'Simcha, Serve the Holy One with Joy: A Siddur.* Ashland OR: Rabbi David Zaslow, 1995.

Rabbi Laura Duhan Kaplan, Ph.D., is an award-winning educator with thirty years' experience teaching philosophy, spirituality, and hatha yoga. She is Director of Inter-Religious Studies at the Vancouver School of Theology, Rabbi Emerita of Or Shalom Synagogue, author of *Family Pictures: A Philosopher Explores the Familiar,* and a Carnegie Foundation U.S. Professor of the Year.

Manufactured by Amazon.ca
Bolton, ON